Let's Ge

SKINNY
COMFORT FOOD

Over **100** comforting recipes

igloobooks

igloobooks

Published in 2017
by Igloo Books Ltd
Cottage Farm
Sywell
NN6 0BJ
www.igloobooks.com

Designed by Nicholas Gage
Edited by Jasmin Peppiatt

Food photography and recipe development
© StockFood, The Food Media Agency
Additional imagery: © iStock / Getty Images

Cover images: © iStock / Getty Images

LEO002 0717
2 4 6 8 10 9 7 5 3 1
ISBN 978-1-78670-919-6

Printed and manufactured in China

Contents

Breakfasts

SERVES: 4 | PREP TIME: 10 MINS | COOKING TIME: 25 MINS

Waffles

250 g / 9 oz / 1 ⅔ cups plain
(all purpose) flour
2 tsp baking powder
2 large eggs
300 ml / 10 ½ fl. oz / 1 ¼ cups milk
2 tbsp melted low-fat butter
sunflower oil, for oiling the waffle maker
icing (confectioner's) sugar to serve

1. Put the oven on a low setting and put an electric waffle maker on to heat.
2. Mix the flour and baking powder in a bowl and make a well in the centre.
3. Break in the eggs and pour in the milk then use a whisk to gradually incorporate all of the flour from around the outside, followed by the melted butter.
4. Spoon some of the batter into the waffle maker and close the lid.
5. Cook for 4 minutes or according to the manufacturer's instructions until golden brown.
6. Repeat until all the batter has been used, keeping the finished batches warm in the oven.
7. Dust the waffles with a little icing sugar before serving, if more sweetness is desired.

MAKES: 4 | PREP TIME: 5 MINS | COOKING TIME: 4 MINS

Smoked Salmon and Cucumber Bagels

4 sesame bagels
125 g / 4 ½ oz / ½ cup low-fat cream cheese
2 tbsp fresh dill, finely chopped
½ lemon, juiced
½ cucumber, thinly sliced
8 slices smoked salmon

1. Heat a griddle pan until smoking hot. Slice the bagels in half and toast them on the griddle for 2 minutes on each side or until nicely marked.
2. Mix the cream cheese with the dill and lemon juice and season to taste with salt and pepper.
3. Spread the bottom half of the bagels with the cream cheese mixture and arrange the cucumber slices and salmon on top.
4. Position the other half of the bagels on top and serve while the bread is still a little warm from the griddle.

SERVES: 1 | PREP TIME: 10 MINS

Fruity Breakfast Granola

300 ml / 10 fl. oz 0% fat yogurt
100 g / 3 ½ oz / ⅔ cup mixed frozen black forest berries, defrosted
100 g / 3 ½ oz / ⅔ cup fresh strawberries
30 g / 1 oz / ⅓ cup granola

1. Place half of the yogurt into a blender and mix with the black forest berries. Blend until smooth and set aside.
2. Blend the other half of the yogurt with 80 g of the strawberries until smooth.
3. Chop the remaining strawberries and place most of them into the bottom of a serving cup. Top with some of the granola and then the strawberry yogurt.
4. Add another layer of granola before topping with the black forest berry yogurt. Finally top with the remaining granola and remaining strawberries.
5. Garnish with further berries and mint leaves if desired.

SERVES: 1 | **PREP TIME: 5 MINS** | **COOKING TIME: 15 MINS**

Fried Cheese and Onion Sandwich

1 tbsp olive oil

½ onion, sliced

1 tbsp Dijon mustard

2 slices of granary bread

50 g / 1 ¾ oz / ½ cup low-fat cheddar cheese, grated

1. Heat the oil in a frying pan over a medium heat and fry the onion for 10 minutes until soft and translucent.

2. While the onions are cooking, spread the bread with the mustard.

3. Once cooked transfer the onions to one of the slices of bread and top with the grated cheese. Place the other slice of bread on top and place the sandwich into the frying pan. Squash down with a spatula and fry until browned, then flip over and cook the other side.

4. Serve immediately.

SERVES: 4 | PREP TIME: 2 MINS | COOKING TIME: 5 MINS

Scrambled Eggs with Rocket

8 large eggs
2 tbsp low-fat butter
50 g rocket leaves
4 English breakfast muffins, halved

1. Gently beat the eggs with a pinch of salt and pepper to break up the yolks.
2. Heat the butter in a non-stick frying pan until sizzling then pour in the eggs.
3. Cook over a low heat, stirring constantly until the eggs scramble.
4. Stir in half of the rocket and divide the mixture between the halved muffins.
5. Serve with extra rocket leaves on the side and a sprinkle of black pepper.

SERVES: 2 | **PREP TIME: 10 MINS** | **COOKING TIME: 20 MINS**

Dairy-free Rice Pudding

1 tbsp dairy-free spread
85 g / 3 oz / ½ cup pudding rice
250 ml / 8 ½ fl. oz almond milk
1 tsp vanilla paste
2 tbsp agave syrup
2 tsp cinnamon
2 tsp nutmeg

1. Melt the dairy-free spread in a large heavy bottomed saucepan before adding the rice, milk, vanilla and half the agave syrup. Stir the mixture together and reduce to a very low heat. Cook gently for 30 minutes or until the rice is tender and the mixture has thickened and become creamy.
2. Spoon into serving bowls before topping with the remaining agave syrup, cinnamon and nutmeg.

SERVES: 4 | **PREP TIME: 2 MINS** | **COOKING TIME: 5 MINS**

Smoked Salmon and Scrambled Egg

8 large eggs
2 tbsp low-fat butter
3 slices smoked salmon, chopped
4 cranberry soda bread rolls, to serve

1. Gently beat the eggs with a pinch of salt and pepper to break up the yolks.
2. Heat the butter in a non-stick frying pan until sizzling then pour in the eggs.
3. Cook over a low heat, stirring constantly until the eggs start to scramble, then stir in the salmon and cook until done to your liking.
4. Spoon onto the bottom half of the rolls and sandwich with the tops.
5. Serve immediately.

SERVES: 1 | PREP TIME: 10 MINS | COOKING TIME: 10 MINS

Breakfast Waffle Sandwich

65 g / 2 ¼ oz / ½ cup plain flour
½ tsp baking powder
½ tsp salt
2 eggs
100 ml / 3 ⅓ fl. oz buttermilk
100 g / 3 ½ oz streaky bacon
50 g curly leaf lettuce

1. Mix together the flour, baking powder and salt in a large mixing bowl. Beat one of the eggs and, using a wooden spoon, mix into the dry ingredients with the buttermilk until you have a smooth batter. Leave to stand for 10 minutes while your waffle iron heats up.

2. Pour the batter into the waffle maker and cook until steam stops rising and the mixture is golden brown.

3. While the waffle is cooking, cut all fat off the bacon then place it under a medium hot grill and cook for 10 minutes, turning once, until crisp.

4. Cut the waffle in half and add the lettuce and top with the cooked bacon. Heat a little oil in a pan and fry the remaining egg adding to the sandwich.

5. Season and top off the sandwich with the remaining half of the waffle.

Chocolate and Banana Granola Pots

200 ml / 7 fl. oz / ¾ cup light cream

200 g / 7 oz dark chocolate, minimum 70% cocoa solids, chopped

4 bananas, sliced

4 tbsp granola

1. Heat the cream until it starts to simmer, then pour it over the chopped chocolate and stir until the mixture has cooled and thickened.
2. Layer the chocolate ganache with the sliced banana inside six glasses and top with a sprinkle of granola.

Pancakes

250 g / 9 oz / 1 ⅔ cups plain (all purpose) flour

2 tsp baking powder

2 large eggs

300 ml / 10 ½ fl. oz / 1 ¼ cups skimmed milk

2 tbsp melted low-fat butter

4 small knobs low-fat butter, to serve

1. Mix the flour and baking powder in a bowl and make a well in the centre.
2. Break in the eggs and pour in the milk then use a whisk to incorporate all of the flour from round the outside.
3. Melt the low-fat butter in a frying pan then whisk into the batter.
4. Put the buttered frying pan back over a low heat. You will need a tablespoon of batter for each pancake and you should be able to cook 4 pancakes at a time.
5. Spoon the batter into the pan and cook for 2 minutes.
6. Turn the pancakes over with a spatula and cook the other side until golden brown and cooked through.
7. Repeat until all the batter has been used.
8. Pile the pancakes onto warm plates and top each one with a knob of low-fat butter.
9. Serve with fruit of your choice.

SERVES: **1** | PREP TIME: **10 MINS**

Egg, Avocado and Rye Bread

1 ripe avocado
2 slices German style rye bread, toasted
½ tsp chilli (chili) flakes
½ lemon, juice only
1 tbsp olive oil
2 eggs
a handful of fresh parsley, finely chopped

1. Peel and destone the avocado before cutting into slices. Place on top of the toast before sprinkling over the chilli flakes and a squeeze of lemon juice.
2. Heat the oil in a frying pan over a medium hot heat. Add the eggs and fry for 3-4 minutes until cooked. Remove from the pan with a spatula and place on top of the avocado before seasoning and garnishing with the chopped parsley.

Lunches and Main Meals

MAKES: 4 | PREP TIME: 5 MINS | COOKING TIME: 5 MINS

Ravioli with Nettle Pesto

450 g / 1 lb fresh ravioli

30 g / 1 oz / 2 cups stinging nettles

1 clove of garlic, crushed

1 lemon, zest finely grated

4 tbsp olive oil

100 g / 3 ½ oz Ricotta Salata, crumbled

1. Cook the ravioli in boiling salted water according to the packet instructions or until al dente.

2. Meanwhile, blanch the nettles in boiling water for 10 seconds then drain well and squeeze out all the liquid.

3. Put them in a blender with the garlic, lemon zest and oil and add a good pinch of salt and pepper, then blend to a smooth sauce.

4. Drain the ravioli and split between 4 warm bowls. Spoon over the nettle pesto and top with the Ricotta Salata.

Sausage, Leek and Potato Casserole

200 g / 7 oz potatoes, peeled

6 reduced fat pork sausages

1 onion, diced

3 leeks, sliced

2 carrots, diced

2 garlic cloves, finely chopped

500 ml / 17 fl. oz reduced salt chicken stock

150 ml / 5 fl. oz light single cream

1 bay leaf

100 g / 3 ½ oz / ½ cup reduced fat cheese, grated

1. Preheat the oven to 180 C. Bring a pan of salted water to the boil and add the potatoes. Cook for 10 minutes so that they are parboiled, drain and set aside.
2. In a large oven proof casserole cook the sausages until browned, about 15 minutes, and remove. Add the onion, leek and carrots and fry them off in the fat from the sausages, add a little oil if necessary. Cook for 10 minutes until softened, then add the garlic and cook for a further minute. Chop the sausages into large pieces and return them to the pan.
3. Add the stock to the pan and bring to the boil and then reduce to a simmer. Add the cream and bay leaf and cook for 5 minutes, seasoning to taste.
4. Slice the potatoes and place them on top of the casserole in layers, before topping with the grated cheese. Place in the oven and cook for 30 minutes, it will be ready once the potatoes are tender.

Caramelized Onion and Mushroom Sandwich

1 tbsp coconut oil

½ onion, sliced

50 g / 1 ¾ oz chestnut mushrooms, sliced

1 garlic clove, minced

50 g / 1 ¾ oz red kale, stem removed and roughly chopped

1 tbsp low-fat crème fraiche

2 slices wholemeal bread, toasted

1. Heat the oil in a large frying pan on a high heat, add the sliced onion and fry for 5 minutes only stirring very rarely. Once the onion has browned and started to turn golden, add the mushroom. Fry for a further 5 minutes until the mushrooms have started to go crispy at the edges.
2. Turn the heat down to a medium high and add the garlic and kale. Cook for a further 2-3 minutes until fragrant and the kale has softened. Stir in the crème fraiche and season with salt and pepper. Place between the toasted bread and serve.

SERVES: 4-6 | PREP TIME: 20 MINS | COOKING TIME: 1 HOUR

Chilli Cheese Nachos

1 tbsp olive oil

1 red onion, diced

500 g / 1 lb lean beef mince

1 tsp chilli powder

1 tsp smoked paprika

1 tsp ground cumin

1 tsp ground coriander

400 g / 14 oz tinned chopped tomatoes

200 ml / 6 ½ fl. oz water

400 g / 14 oz tinned kidney beans, drained

200 g / 7 oz unsalted tortilla chips

50 g / 1 ¾ oz jalapeno peppers in brine

100 g / 3 ½ oz / 1 cup lighter Cheddar cheese, grated

100 g / 3 ½ oz / 1 cup lighter Red Leicester, grated

1. Heat the oil over a medium high heat in a large casserole. Add the onion and cook for 5-10 minutes until softened. Add the beef mince and brown before adding the chilli powder, paprika, cumin and coriander. Fry for a further minute until fragrant before adding the chopped tomatoes and water. Bring to the boil and then reduce to a simmer and cover and cook for 45 minutes, adding the beans for the last 10 minutes.

2. Preheat the oven to 180°C (160°C fan) / 350F / gas 4. Put the tortilla chips in a cast iron skillet or oven proof dish, top with a generous helping of the chilli, jalapenos and grated cheese before placing in the oven.

3. Bake for 10-15 minutes so that the cheese has melted and started to brown.

4. Serve with guacamole and fresh salsa.

SERVES: 2 | **PREP TIME: 10 MINS** | **COOKING TIME: 10 MINS**

Pad Thai Noodles

200 g / 7 oz raw king prawns
a small bunch of coriander, stalks finely chopped.
½ red onion, sliced
1 tsp chilli (chili) flakes
2 packs of straight to wok pad thai noodles
100 g / 3 ½ oz beansprouts
1 egg, beaten
1 lime, juiced
1 tbsp fish sauce
3 spring onions (scallions), sliced
1 tbsp roasted peanuts, chopped

1. Heat a wok to a high heat and add the prawns and coriander stalks and fry until the prawns turn pink, roughly 3 minutes. Add the red onion and chilli flakes and fry for a further minute keeping everything in the pan moving.
2. Add the noodles, beansprouts, egg, lime and fish sauce and continue to cook for a further 2-3 minutes until the egg is cooked and the noodles have been heated through.
3. Divide between two serving bowls and top with the chopped coriander leaves, spring onions and chopped peanuts and serve with lime wedges.

SERVES: 4 | PREP TIME: 10 MINS | COOKING TIME: 45 MINS

Sausage and Bean Casserole

1 tbsp olive oil
6 low-fat pork sausages
2 rashers back bacon, chopped
1 onion, diced
1 celery stick, finely sliced
2 garlic cloves, chopped
250 g / 9 oz butterbeans, soaked overnight
500 ml / 17 fl. oz chicken stock
2 sprigs thyme
2 bay leaves
a small bunch fresh parsley, chopped

1. In a large casserole dish, heat the oil over a medium heat. Add the sausages to the pan and fry for 12-15 minutes until browned. Remove and set aside. Add the bacon to the pan and fry for 3 minutes before adding the onion and celery. Continue to fry for a further 5 minutes until translucent, before adding the garlic and frying for 1 minute.
2. Meanwhile, drain the beans and place into a pan of rapidly boiling salted water for 10 minutes before draining and rinsing.
3. Slice the sausages and return to the casserole with the drained beans. Pour in the chicken stock and add the thyme and bay leaves. Bring to the boil and reduce heat to a simmer for 15 minutes, or until the beans are cooked.
4. Season and top with the chopped parsley before serving.

SERVES: **1** | PREP TIME: **10 MINS**

Seafood Salad Sandwich

100 g / 3 ½ oz white and brown crab meat

50 g / 1 ¾ oz king prawn, cooked and chopped

2 tbsp low-fat mayonnaise

1 tsp ketchup

a pinch of cayenne

½ lemon, juiced

1 spring onion (scallion), sliced

2 slices wholemeal bread

2 reduced fat cheese slices

1. In a bowl, combine the crab, prawn, mayonnaise, ketchup, cayenne, lemon juice and onion. Mix together until well mixed and season with salt and black pepper to taste.

2. Toast the bread and then top with a cheese slice on each. Add the seafood mixture to one of the halves of the sandwich and top with the other.

Sausages and Baked Onion Gravy

8 reduced fat sausages
2 red onions, cut into wedges
2 tbsp runny honey
1 tbsp Dijon mustard
250 ml / 9 fl. oz / 1 cup chicken stock

1. Preheat the oven to 180°C (160° fan) / 350F / gas 4.
2. Arrange the sausages and onion wedges in a baking dish and season with salt and pepper.
3. Mix the honey with the mustard then slowly incorporate the chicken stock.
4. Pour the mixture over the sausages and onions then transfer the dish to the oven.
5. Bake for 30 minutes, turning the sausages and stirring the onions half way through.

Chicken Korma

450 g / 1 lb skinless chicken breast, cubed
2 tbsp korma curry powder
2 tbsp olive oil
1 onion, finely chopped
1 red chilli (chili), finely chopped
2 cloves of garlic, crushed
200 g / 7 oz / 1 cup canned
    tomatoes, chopped
400 ml / 14 fl. oz / 1 ⅔ cups coconut milk
4 tbsp ground almonds
2 tbsp mango chutney

1. Mix the chicken breast pieces with the curry powder and leave to marinate for 30 minutes.
2. Heat the oil in a large saucepan and fry the onion and chilli for 3 minutes, stirring occasionally.
3. Add the garlic and cook for 2 minutes or until the mustard seeds start to pop.
4. Add the chicken and cook for 4 minutes, stirring occasionally, until it starts to colour on the outside.
5. Add the chopped tomatoes, coconut milk, ground almonds and mango chutney and bring to a gentle simmer.
6. Cook the curry for 35 minutes, stirring occasionally, until the chicken is tender and the sauce has thickened.

SERVES: 4 | PREP TIME: **10 MINS** | COOKING TIME: **45 MINS**

Toad in the Hole

1 tbsp olive oil
6 venison sausages
150 g / 4 oz / 1 cup plain flour
¼ tsp salt
1 egg
300 ml / 10 fl. oz / 1 ¼ cups skimmed milk

1. Preheat the oven to 220°C (200°C fan) / 425F / gas 7. Place a medium-sized baking dish into the oven with the oil to heat. After 2 minutes, add the sausages and cook for 10-15 minutes, turning occasionally, until browned.
2. While the sausages are cooking, mix the flour and salt in a medium sized mixing bowl. Using a wooden spoon, beat in the egg and enough milk to form a stiff, smooth batter. Set aside for 5 minutes and then gradually beat in the remaining milk. Cover and set aside until needed.
3. Remove the dish with the sausages from the oven and, while still hot, pour the batter into the dish. Place back into the oven and reduce the heat to 180°C / 350F / gas 4 and bake for 30 minutes until the batter has risen and turned golden brown.
4. Remove from the oven and serve immediately with green vegetables.

Vegetable Pilaf

3 tbsp oil
1 cinnamon stick
4 cardamom pods
4 cloves
1 onion, sliced
1 tsp turmeric
1 large carrot, cut into batons
1 courgette sliced
250 g / 9 oz mushrooms, sliced
250 g / 9 oz / 1 ¼ cups basmati rice,
   washed and soaked
600 ml / 20 fl. oz low salt vegetable stock
400 g / 14 oz can of chick peas, drained

1. Heat the oil in a large heavy based saucepan. Fry the cinnamon, cardamom and cloves for a few seconds until fragrant. Add the onion and cook until golden and translucent.

2. Add the turmeric and fry for a few seconds before adding the vegetables. Fry for 5 minutes stirring regularly. Add the drained rice and fry for a further 5 minutes until coated in the spices.

3. Pour the stock into the pan and bring to the boil. Reduce the heat and simmer, uncovered, for 10 minutes until most of the liquid has been absorbed and the rice is tender. Add the chick peas to the pan and warm through for a further 4-5 minutes. Mix through the rice and check that all the liquid has been absorbed.

4. Spoon into serving dishes and serve with chapatti breads.

Macaroni Cheese

350 g / 12 oz macaroni pasta
2 tbsp low-fat butter
1 garlic clove, finely chopped
1 tsp English mustard
3 tbsp plain flour
500 ml / 17 fl. oz skimmed milk
350 g / 12 oz / 3 ½ cups low-fat mature
   Cheddar, grated

1. Cook the pasta as per the packets instructions so that it is slightly al dente, drain well and set aside

2. In a saucepan, melt the butter and add the garlic. Fry for 1 minute until fragrant before stirring in the mustard. Stir in the flour and cook for a further minute before gradually adding the milk, whisking constantly. Once all the milk has been added, continue to cook the thickened sauce for 5 minutes whisking constantly. Remove from the heat and stir in 250 g of the grated cheese and season.

3. Preheat the oven to 200°C (180°C fan) / 400F / gas 6. Combine the drained pasta with the cheese sauce before pouring into an oven proof dish. Sprinkle over the remaining grated cheese and bake in the oven for 20 minutes until crisp and golden.

SERVES: 4 | PREP TIME: 15 MINS | COOKING TIME: 30 MINS

Buttermilk Biscuits and Gravy

30 g / 1 oz / ⅓ cup butter
170 g / 6 oz / 1 ¼ cups flour
1 tsp salt
1 tsp baking powder
½ tsp bicarbonate of soda
150 ml / 5 fl. oz buttermilk
1 tbsp rapeseed oil
500 g / 1 lb lean pork mince
½ onion, finely chopped
3 tbsp plain flour
450 ml / 15 fl. oz skimmed milk
sea salt and freshly ground black pepper
tabasco (optional)

1. Preheat the oven to 220°C (200°C fan) / 425F / gas 7, lightly grease a baking tray.
2. In a mixing bowl, mix the flour, salt, baking powder and bicarbonate. Using your fingertips rub in the butter until rough breadcrumbs form. Stir in the buttermilk until a soft dough forms.
3. Knead on a floured surface for 1 minute, roll out to around 2 cm thickness. Using a 2-inch pastry cutter, cut out and place onto the baking tray. Bake in the oven for 15 minutes until a skewer inserted into the centre of a scones comes out clean.
4. While the biscuits are baking, heat the oil in a large frying pan and add the pork mince and onion. Fry for 10 minutes until browned before adding the flour and stirring through for 2 minutes. Gradually add the milk mixing it in completely after each addition until you have a thick gravy.
5. Season and add tabasco, if desired.
6. Halve the freshly baked biscuits and top with the hot gravy.

Roast Chicken with Lemon

1 tbsp olive oil
4 large chicken thighs
sea salt
2 shallots, sliced
1 preserved lemon, sliced
1 large piece of ginger, peeled and sliced
    into batons
a handful of black olives
a handful of coriander (cilantro),
    roughly chopped
1 lemon, juiced

1. Preheat the oven to 200°C (180°C fan) / 400F / gas 6. In a cast iron skillet, heat the oil over a high heat. Season the skin of the chicken and place skin side down in the pan. Cook for 2 minutes before lowering the heat to medium high and continuing to cook the chicken skin side down for 10 minutes so that the skin is golden brown.
2. Turn the chicken over and add the shallots, lemon, ginger and olives to the pan. Cook for a further 2 minutes. Add 50 ml of water to the pan before transferring to the oven and roasting for 12-15 minutes until the juices of the meat run clear.
3. Remove from the oven and sprinkle over the coriander and lemon juice before serving.

Paella with Chorizo

1 tbsp olive oil
100 g / 3.5 oz chorizo, sliced
1 onion, diced
1 red pepper, diced
2 garlic cloves, minced
1 tsp paprika
250 g / 9 oz / 1 ¼ cups paella rice
500 ml / 17 fl. oz reduced salt chicken stock
1 tsp saffron
200 g / 7oz mixed seafood, cooked
100 g / 3.5 oz octopus, tinned
150 g / 5 oz peas, cooked and drained
1 lemon, juiced
1 bunch flat leaf parsley, finely chopped
sea salt and black pepper

1. In a wide pan, heat the olive oil over a medium heat and fry the chorizo for 2 minutes until browned. Remove with a slotted spoon and set aside.
2. Add the onion and fry for 3 minutes before adding the peppers and cooking for a further 2 minutes. Add the garlic and paprika and fry for a further minute. Stir the rice into the pan and pour in the stock and add the saffron, bring to the boil and then reduce and simmer for 15-20 minutes, stirring occasionally, until the stock has been absorbed and the rice is cooked.
3. Return the chorizo to the pan and add the seafood, octopus and peas and gently heat. Before serving, add the lemon juice, stir through the parsley and season.
4. Serve with lemon wedges.

SERVES: 4 | PREP TIME: 15 MINS | COOKING TIME: 30 MINS

Lamb Stuffed Peppers

1 tbsp olive oil

1 onion, diced

2 garlic cloves, crushed

500 g / 1 lb lean lamb mince,
  10% fat

1 tsp dried oregano

1 tsp dried basil

200 g / 7 oz / 1 cup pearl barley

400 g / 14 oz chopped tomatoes

250 ml / 8 ½ fl. oz water

4 large red peppers

4 large red peppers

50 g / 1 ¾ oz / ½ cup feta cheese

a handful of chopped mint

1. Heat the oil in a large heavy based pan over a medium high heat. Add the onions and fry until slightly golden and translucent. Add the garlic and fry for a further minute before adding the mince. Fry the lamb mince for 5 minutes until browned and add the dried herbs.

2. Add the pearl barley to the lamb mince and mix through before adding the chopped tomatoes and water. Bring to the boil and then lower to a simmer and cook for 45 minutes or until the barley is softened.

3. Preheat the oven to 180°C (160°C fan) / 350F / gas 4. Cut the top off the peppers and carefully scoop out the seeds and pith. Fill each of the peppers with the lamb mixture and place them into an ovenproof dish. Crumble over the feta and mint before replacing the tops of the peppers.

4. Bake into the oven for 30 minutes or until the peppers are charred and soft when a knife is inserted and serve immediately.

Sausages with Champ Potatoes

2 tbsp olive oil

12 sausages

900 g / 2 lb potatoes, peeled and cubed

250 ml / 9 fl. oz / 1 cup whole milk

150 g / 5 ½ oz / ⅔ cup butter, cubed

4 spring onions (scallions), chopped

1. Heat the oil in a frying pan and fry the sausages very gently for 20 minutes, turning regularly.
2. Meanwhile, cook the potatoes in boiling salted water for 10 minutes or until tender all the way through.
3. Tip the potatoes into a colander and leave to drain.
4. Put the saucepan back on the heat and add the milk and butter.
5. Heat until the milk starts to simmer then return the potatoes to the pan.
6. Mash the potatoes until smooth then stir in the spring onions and season well with salt and pepper.

Crab Cakes

4 tbsp plain (all purpose) flour

1 egg, beaten

75 g / 2 ½ oz / ½ cup panko breadcrumbs

450 g / 1 lb / 2 cups leftover
  mashed potato

200 g / 7 oz / 1 ¼ cup fresh crab meat

2 spring onions, finely chopped

2 tbsp fresh dill, finely chopped

sunflower oil for deep-frying

1. Put the flour, egg and panko breadcrumbs in 3 separate bowls.
2. Mix the mashed potato with the crab, spring onions and dill then shape it into 16 small patties.
3. Dip the crab cakes alternately in the flour, egg and breadcrumbs and shake off any excess.
4. Heat the oil in a deep fat fryer, according to the manufacturer's instructions, to a temperature of 180°C.
5. Lower the crab cakes in the fryer basket and cook for 4 minutes or until crisp and golden brown.
6. Tip the crab cakes into a kitchen paper lined bowl to remove any excess oil.

SERVES: 4 | PREP TIME: 2 MINS | COOKING TIME: 1 HOUR 30 MINS

Sweet Potato Cottage Pie

2 tbsp olive oil
1 small onion, finely chopped
2 cloves of garlic, crushed
450 g / 1 lb / 2 cups minced beef
400 g / 14 oz / 1 ¾ cups canned
    tomatoes, chopped
400 ml / 14 fl. oz / 1 ⅔ cups beef stock

FOR THE TOPPING
2 large sweet potatoes
50 g / 1 ¾ oz / ¼ cup butter
2 tsp fresh thyme leaves

1. Preheat the oven to 200°C (180° fan) / 400F / gas 6.
2. Bake the sweet potatoes in their skins for 45 or until a skewer inserted slides in easily.
3. Meanwhile, heat the oil in a large saucepan and fry the onion for 3 minutes, stirring occasionally.
4. Add the garlic and cook for 2 minutes, then add the mince.
5. Fry the mince until it starts to brown then add the chopped tomatoes and stock and bring to a gentle simmer.
6. Cook for 1 hour, stirring occasionally, until the mince is tender and the sauce has thickened a little.
7. When the sweet potatoes are ready, peel off and discard the skins and mash the flesh with the butter and thyme leaves.
8. Spoon the mince mixture into a large baking dish then top with the mashed sweet potatoes.
9. Use a fork to level the surface and make stripes in the potato then bake in the oven for 20 minutes or until golden brown.

SERVES: 4 | **PREP TIME: 5 MINS** | **COOKING TIME: 30 MINS**

Chunky Bacon and Vegetable Soup

2 tbsp olive oil

2 tbsp butter

1 onion, finely chopped

2 cloves of garlic, crushed

2 medium potatoes, cubed

3 carrots, cubed

1 litre / 1 pint 15 fl. oz / 4 cups
vegetable stock

150 g / 5 ½ oz / 1 cup peas, defrosted
if frozen

4 rashers streaky bacon

a few sprigs of chervil to serve

1. Heat the oil and butter in a saucepan and fry the onion for 5 minutes or until softened.
2. Add the garlic, potatoes and carrots to the pan and cook for 2 more minutes, then stir in the vegetable stock and bring to the boil.
3. Simmer for 12 minutes then add the peas and simmer for a further 5 minutes.
4. While the peas are cooking, cook the bacon under a hot grill until crispy then chop into large pieces.
5. Stir the bacon into the soup, add salt and pepper to taste and garnish with chervil.

SERVES: 4 | PREP TIME: 5 MINS | COOKING TIME: 20 MINS

Vegetable Soup

2 tbsp olive oil

2 leeks, sliced

2 cloves of garlic, crushed

4 spring onions, chopped

2 courgettes, chopped

1 red pepper, sliced

1 orange pepper, chopped

150 g / 5 ½ oz / 1 cup broad beans, defrosted if frozen

1 litre / 1 pint 15 fl. oz / 4 cups vegetable stock

a few sprigs of flat leaf parsley to serve

1. Heat the oil in a saucepan and fry the leeks for 5 minutes or until softened.
2. Add the garlic and vegetables to the pan and cook for 2 more minutes, then stir in the vegetable stock and bring to the boil.
3. Simmer for 10 minutes then season to taste with salt and pepper.
4. Ladle the soup into 4 warm bowls and garnish with parsley.

Bacon and Egg Scones

225 g / 8 oz / 1 ½ cups self-raising flour
55 g / 2 oz / ¼ cup low-fat butter
150 ml / 5 fl. oz / ⅔ cup skimmed milk

FOR THE FILLING
4 large eggs
4 rashers streaky bacon
4 tbsp light mayonnaise
cress to garnish

1. Preheat the oven to 220°C (200° fan) / 425F / gas 7 and oil a large baking sheet.
2. Sieve the flour into a bowl and rub in the butter until the mixture resembles fine breadcrumbs. Stir in enough milk to bring the mixture together into a soft dough.
3. Flatten the dough with your hands on a floured work surface until 2.5 cm (1 in) thick.
4. Use a pastry cutter to cut out 12 circles and transfer them to the baking sheet.
5. Bake in the oven for 10–15 minutes or until golden brown and cooked through. Transfer the scones to a wire rack to cool a little while you make the filling.
6. Boil the eggs for 6 minutes then drain and plunge into cold water for 4 minutes.
7. Meanwhile, grill the bacon for 3 minutes on each side or until crisp, then roughly chop. Peel the eggs and mash them with a fork then mix with the bacon pieces and mayonnaise.
8. Split open the scones and fill with the bacon and egg mayonnaise and a sprinkle of cress.

Chicken Fajitas

450 g / 1 lb chicken breast, sliced
2 tbsp fajita seasoning mix
2 tbsp sunflower oil
1 onion, sliced
1 red pepper, sliced
1 yellow pepper, sliced
1 green pepper, sliced
8 soft flour tortillas
guacamole to serve

1. Toss the chicken with the seasoning mix and leave to marinate for 30 minutes.
2. Heat the oil in a large frying pan and stir-fry the chicken for 4 minutes.
3. Add the onions and peppers and stir fry for a further 4 minutes, then divide the mixture between the tortillas.
4. Roll up the fajitas and serve with guacamole for dipping.

MAKES: 6 | PREP TIME: 10 MINS | COOKING TIME: 30–35 MINS

Mini Fish Pies

450 g / 1 lb potatoes, peeled and cubed
500 ml / 17 ½ fl. oz / 2 cups milk
1 bay leaf
400 g / 14 oz smoked haddock fillet
4 tbsp low-fat butter
2 tbsp plain flour

1. Preheat the oven to 200°C (180° fan) / 400F / gas 6.
2. Cook the potatoes in boiling salted water for 12 minutes or until tender then drain well. Meanwhile, put the milk and bay leaf in a small saucepan and bring to a simmer.
3. Lay the haddock in a snugly-fitting dish and pour the hot milk over the top. Cover the dish with clingfilm and leave to stand for 10 minutes.
4. Heat half of the butter in a small saucepan and stir in the flour.
5. Reserve 2 tablespoons of the haddock milk for the potatoes and strain the rest into the butter and flour mixture, stirring constantly. Cook until the sauce is thick and smooth.
6. Remove any skin and bones from the haddock then flake the flesh into the white sauce. Season to taste with salt and black pepper then divide the mixture between 6 individual pie dishes.
7. Mash the potatoes with the reserved milk and remaining butter and spoon it on top of the haddock.
8. Bake the pies for 15 minutes or until the topping is golden brown.

Sardine and Egg Panini

120 g / 4 oz canned sardines in oil
2 large ciabatta rolls, halved
2 boiled eggs, sliced
rocket (arugula) to serve

1. Put an electric panini press on to heat.
2. Mash the sardines into their oil with a fork and spread them over the bottom halves of the rolls.
3. Top with the boiled egg slices, season with salt and pepper, then sandwich together with the top of the rolls.
4. Toast the panini for 3 minutes or according to the manufacturer's instructions.
5. Cut the panini into four pieces each and serve two pieces per person with some rocket on the side.

Roast Beef Toasted Sandwich

8 slices white bread
4 tbsp light mayonnaise
1 tsp Dijon mustard
1 tsp wholegrain mustard
8 slices rare roast beef
4 tbsp French tarragon leaves

1. Toast the bread in a toaster or under a hot grill.
2. Mix the mayonnaise with the mustards and season with a little black pepper.
3. Spread the mustard mayonnaise over the toast and top four of the slices with the beef.
4. Scatter over the tarragon leaves, then sandwich with the rest of the toast and cut in half on the diagonal.

Cream Cheese and Salad Rolls

4 oat-topped wholemeal rolls, halved
125 g / 4 ½ oz / ½ cup cream cheese
1 medium tomato, sliced
½ cucumber, sliced
4 lettuce leaves

1. Spread the bottom half of the rolls thickly with cream cheese and arrange the tomato, cucumber and lettuce on top.
2. Sandwich with the other half of the rolls and serve immediately.

SERVES: 8 | PREP TIME: 20 MINS | COOKING TIME: 45 MINS

Moussaka

180 ml / 6 fl. oz cup olive oil

2 large aubergine (eggplant), sliced

1 onion, diced

3 garlic cloves, finely chopped

500 g / 1 lb lean lamb mince

400 g / 14 oz tin of chopped tomatoes

1 tsp chopped sage

1 tsp chopped rosemary

500 ml / 17 fl. oz low-fat yogurt

2 eggs, beaten

1 tsp grated nutmeg

1 lemon, juice and zest

50 g / 1.7 oz / ½ cup low-fat feta cheese, crumbled

100 g / 3 ½ oz cherry tomatoes, halved.

50 g / 1 ¾ oz / ½ cup parmesan cheese, grated

1. Heat half the oil in a large heavy bottomed frying pan over a medium high heat. Coat the sliced aubergine in flour and fry on each side until golden brown. Place on kitchen paper to drain.

2. Preheat the oven to 190°C (170°C fan) / 375F / gas 5. Add the remaining oil to the pan and fry the onion for 5 minutes until golden brown. Add the garlic and for a further minute before adding the lamb mince. Fry for 10 minutes until browned then add the tomatoes. Bring to the boil then simmer for 20 minutes and add the chopped herbs.

3. In a bowl, mix together the yogurt, egg, nutmeg, lemon and feta cheese, season and set aside.

4. In an ovenproof dish, add a layer of lamb before topping with a layer of aubergine, repeat this again before topping with the yogurt mix. Add the remaining aubergine and chopped tomatoes before sprinkling with the cheese. Bake for 30 minutes or until the top is golden brown and the yogurt mixture has set.

Beef and Butterbean Stew

4 tbsp olive oil
800 g / 1 lb 12 oz braising steak, diced
1 onion, finely chopped
4 cloves of garlic, finely chopped
400 g / 14 oz / 2 cups canned
　tomatoes, chopped
400 ml / 14 fl. oz / 1 ⅔ cups good quality
　beef stock
400 g / 14 oz / 2 cups canned
　butterbeans, drained
1 head of broccoli, broken into florets
fresh tomato and chilli (chili) relish to serve

1. Preheat the oven to 140°C (120° fan) / 275F / gas 1. Heat half of the oil in a large cast iron casserole dish and sear the beef on all sides until well browned.
2. Remove the meat from the pan, add the rest of the oil and fry the onions and garlic for 5 minutes. Add the tomatoes and stock and bring to a simmer then return the beef to the pan.
3. Cover the casserole with a lid, transfer it to the oven and cook for 3 hours.
4. Around 30 minutes before the end of the cooking time, stir in the butterbeans and broccoli and season the sauce with salt and pepper as necessary.
5. Ladle into bowls and top with a spoonful of fresh tomato and chilli relish.

Thai Green Curry

250 g / 9 oz / 1 ¼ cups Thai jasmine rice
1 tsp groundnut oil
2 tbsp Thai green curry paste
1 aubergine, diced
4 kaffir lime leaves
1 stick lemongrass, bruised
1 tbsp fish sauce
1 can low-fat coconut milk
500 g / 1 lb turkey breast, cut into strips
a small bunch of coriander (cilantro), stalks
　and leaves
1 fresh green chilli (chili) sliced
1 lime

1. In a saucepan, cook the rice as per the packet instructions and keep warm whilst you prepare the curry.
2. In a large wok, heat the oil over a medium high heat. Add the curry paste and fry for 2 minutes until fragrant. Add the aubergine, lime leaves, lemongrass and fish sauce continuing to fry for a further 2 minutes. If the ingredients are looking a little dry add a splash of the coconut milk.
3. Pour in the coconut milk before adding the turkey. Bring to the boil and then reduce to a simmer for 12-15 minutes, adding the chopped coriander stalks, until the meat is cooked.
4. Serve in a bowl and garnish with the chopped coriander leaves, chilli and a lime wedge.

SERVES: 4 | PREP TIME: 10 MINS | COOKING TIME: 3 HOURS 30 MINS

Homemade Baked Beans with Sausages

400 g / 14 oz / 2 ⅔ cups dried haricot
  beans, soaked overnight

1 large ham hock

400 g / 14 oz / 2 ⅔ cups canned
  tomatoes, chopped

2 tbsp vegetable oil

8 pork sausages

2 tbsp flat leaf parsley,
  finely chopped

1. Preheat the oven to 150°C (130° fan) /
   300F / gas 2.
2. Drain the beans and put them in a
   large cast iron casserole dish with the
   ham hock and canned tomatoes, then
   add enough cold water to cover it all
   by 5 cm (2 in)
3. Bring the pan to the boil on the stove,
   then cover with a lid and transfer to
   the oven for 4 hours, topping up with
   water if it starts to get too dry.
4. Heat the oil in a frying pan and brown
   the sausage all over. Stir the baked
   beans and taste for seasoning, then
   add the sausages and return to the
   oven for a further 30 minutes.
5. Slice the ham off the bone and
   divide between four warm bowls
   with the sausages and beans,
   then sprinkle with parsley.

MAKES: 2 | **PREP TIME: 2 HOURS 30 MINS** | COOKING TIME: **10-12 MINS**

Vegetable Pizza

400 g / 14 oz / 2 ⅔ cups strong white bread flour, plus extra for dusting

½ tsp easy blend dried yeast

2 tsp caster (superfine) sugar

1 tsp fine sea salt

1 tbsp olive oil

4 tbsp tomato pizza sauce

½ aubergine (eggplant), chopped

1 courgette (zucchini), chopped

1 red pepper, chopped

1 yellow pepper, chopped

100 g / 3 ½ oz preserved artichokes in oil, drained and chopped

150 g / 5 ½ oz mozzarella, grated

2 tsp dried oregano

1. Mix together the flour, yeast, sugar and salt and stir the oil into 140 ml of warm water.
2. Stir the liquid into the dry ingredients then knead on a lightly oiled surface for 10 minutes or until smooth and elastic.
3. Leave the dough to rest covered with oiled clingfilm for 1-2 hours until doubled in size. Preheat the oven to 220°C (200° fan) / 425F/ gas 7 and grease 2 non-stick baking trays.
4. Knead the dough for 2 more minutes then divide in half and roll out into 2 circles.
5. Transfer the bases to the baking trays, spread with pizza sauce and sprinkle with cheese.
6. Arrange the vegetables on top and sprinkle with oregano then bake for 10-12 minutes or until the base is cooked through underneath.

Steak Stew

2 tbsp olive oil
1 onion, finely chopped
1 carrot, finely chopped
1 celery stick, finely chopped
1 red chilli (chili), finely chopped
2 cloves of garlic, crushed
½ tsp cayenne pepper
450 g / 1 lb / 2 cups braising steak, cubed
400 g / 14 oz / 1 ⅔ cups beef stock
400 g / 14 oz / 1 ¾ cups canned kidney
  beans, drained
400 g / 14 oz / 1 ¾ cups canned
  sweetcorn, drained
2 courgettes (zucchini), sliced

1. Heat the oil in a large saucepan and fry the onion, carrot, celery and chilli for 3 minutes, stirring occasionally.
2. Add the garlic and cayenne and cook for 2 minutes, then add the beef.
3. Fry the beef until it starts to brown then add the stock and bring to a gentle simmer.
4. Cook for 1 hour, stirring occasionally, then add the kidney beans, sweetcorn and courgette and cook for a further 30 minutes.
5. Taste for seasoning and add salt and freshly ground black pepper as necessary.

Chicken and Black Bean Stew

1 tbsp olive oil
4 chicken thighs, skinless and boneless
100 g / 3 ½ oz chorizo, sliced
1 onion, diced
2 garlic cloves, finely chopped
2 red peppers, roughly chopped
400 g / 14 oz chopped tomatoes
200 ml / 7 fl. oz water
400 g / 14 oz tinned black beans, drained
a handful of chopped parsley

1. Heat the oil over a medium heat in a large heavy bottomed pan. Roughly chop the chicken and brown in the hot oil, remove with a slotted spoon and set aside.
2. Add the sliced chorizo to the pan and fry for 2-3 minutes until the oil has turned golden yellow, remove from the pan and set aside with the chicken.
3. Add the onion to the pan and cook for 2-3 minutes until translucent, add a little more oil if needed. Add the garlic and fry for a further minute before adding the peppers. Cook for a further 2-3 minutes before adding the chopped tomatoes and water. Return the chicken and chorizo to the pan and bring to the boil before turning down to a simmer. Cover and cook for 20 minutes, adding the beans for the final 5 minutes.
4. Season with salt and black pepper to taste and serve in the pan with the chopped parsley scattered on the surface.

SERVES: 4 | PREP TIME: 5 MINS | COOKING TIME: 30 MINS

Tomato and Thyme Soup

2 tbsp olive oil

1 onion, finely chopped

4 cloves of garlic, crushed

2 tbsp thyme leaves

450 g / 1 lb ripe tomatoes, diced

500 ml / 17 ½ fl. oz / 2 cups
   vegetable stock

1. Heat the oil in a saucepan and fry the onion for 8 minutes or until softened.
2. Add the garlic and half of the thyme to the pan and cook for 2 more minutes, then stir in the tomatoes and vegetable stock and bring to the boil.
3. Simmer for 20 minutes then blend until smooth with a liquidizer or immersion blender.
4. Taste the soup and adjust the seasoning with salt and pepper, then ladle into bowls and sprinkle with the rest of the thyme.

SERVES: 4 | PREP TIME: 5 MINS | COOKING TIME: 1 HOUR 15 MINS

Lamb and Summer Vegetable Stew

4 tbsp olive oil

450 g / 1 lb lamb leg, cubed

1 onion, diced

3 cloves of garlic, finely chopped

200 g / 7 oz / 1 cup canned tomatoes, chopped

600 ml / 1 pint / 2 ½ cups good quality lamb stock

½ Japanese aubergine (eggplant), sliced

2 courgettes (zucchini), cubed

150 g / 5 ½ oz green (string) beans

a few sprigs of flat leaf parsley to serve

1. Heat half of the oil in a large saucepan and sear the lamb on all sides until well browned.
2. Remove the lamb from the pan, add the rest of the oil and fry the onions and garlic for 5 minutes.
3. Add the tomatoes and stock and bring to a simmer then return the lamb to the pan.
4. Cover the pan with a lid and simmer gently for 45 minutes.
5. Add the aubergine, courgette and beans and simmer for a further 15 minutes then taste the sauce for seasoning and adjust with salt and pepper.
6. Garnish with parsley just before serving.

SERVES: 4 | PREP TIME: 5 MINS | COOKING TIME: 2 HOURS

Lamb Shank and Vegetable Tagines

4 lamb shanks
12 baby carrots, peeled
8 spring onions, trimmed
4 small turnips, peeled
6 new potatoes, peeled and halved
400 ml / 14 fl. oz / 1 ⅔ cups lamb stock
2 cloves of garlic, crushed
1 lemon, juiced
1 tbsp flat leaf parsley, chopped

1. Preheat the oven to 180°C (160° fan) / 350F / gas 4.
2. Put each lamb shank in an individual tagine and divide the vegetables between them.
3. Mix the lamb stock with the garlic and lemon juice and season well with salt and pepper, then pour it over the lamb and put on the lids.
4. Transfer the tagines to the oven and bake for 2 hours.
5. Remove the lids and sprinkle with parsley before serving.

MAKES: 4 | PREP TIME: 45 MINS | COOKING TIME: 45 MINS

Mini Chicken and Vegetable Pies

2 tbsp butter
1 onion, chopped
1 potato, chopped
1 tsp plain (all purpose) flour
250 ml / 9 fl. oz / 1 cup milk
200 g / 7 oz cooked chicken breast, cubed
75 g / 2 ½ oz / ½ cup peas, defrosted if frozen
75 g / 2 ½ oz / 1 cup button
  mushrooms, quartered
6 cherry tomatoes, quartered

FOR THE PASTRY
100 g / 3 ½ oz / ½ cup butter, cubed
  and chilled
200 g / 7 oz / 1 ⅓ cups plain
  (all purpose) flour

1. To make the pastry, rub the butter into the flour until the mixture resembles fine breadcrumbs. Stir in just enough cold water to bring the pastry together into a pliable dough then chill for 30 minutes.
2. Preheat the oven to 200°C (180° fan) / 400F / gas 6. Heat the butter in a saucepan and fry the onion and potato for 5 minutes without colouring. Sprinkle in the flour, then stir in the milk and bubble until it thickens slightly.
3. Add the chicken, peas, mushrooms and tomatoes to the pan and heat through, then season to taste.
4. Roll out the pastry on a floured surface and cut out 4 circles. Divide the filling between four pie dishes and brush the rims with water. Top each pie with a pastry lid and crimp the edges to seal. Bake the pies for 25 minutes.

MAKES: **6** | PREP TIME: **10 MINS** | COOKING TIME: **1 HOUR 45 MINS**

Mini Sausage Cassoulet

400 g / 14 oz / 2 ⅔ cups dried haricot beans, soaked overnight

3 litres / 5 pints 6 fl. oz / 12 cups good quality chicken stock

2 tbsp olive oil

6 good quality pork sausages

1 morteau sausage, sliced

100 g / 3 ½ oz chorizo, cubed

2 cloves of garlic, crushed

50 g / 1 ¾ oz / ⅔ cup breadcrumbs

a few sprigs of parsley to garnish

1. Put the beans in a large saucepan with the stock and simmer gently for 1 hour.
2. Meanwhile, heat the oil in a frying pan and brown the sausages all over, then cut them in half.
3. Preheat the oven to 150°C (130° fan) / 300F / gas 2.
4. Drain the beans and reserve the stock then stir in the sausages, morteau, chorizo and garlic.
5. Divide the mixture between 6 mini casserole dishes, then sprinkle with breadcrumbs.
6. Bake the cassoulets for 45 minutes, topping up with extra stock if necessary.

Couscous and Vegetable Gratin

300 g / 10 ½ oz / 1 ¾ cups couscous
2 tbsp olive oil
1 carrot, diced
100 g / 3 ½ oz green (string) beans, chopped
100 g / 3 ½ oz / ⅔ cup podded baby
   broad beans
2 tbsp pine nuts
2 tbsp flat leaf parsley, finely chopped

FOR THE TOPPING
450 g / 1 lb carrots, peeled and chopped
450 g / 1 lb broccoli, broken into florets
100 g / 3 ½ oz / ½ cup butter
50 g / 1 ¾ oz / ½ cup Emmental, grated

1. Preheat the oven to 200°C (180° fan) / 400F / gas 6. To make the topping, cook the carrots and broccoli in separate pans of salted water for 10 minutes, or until they are tender, then drain well. Add half of the butter to each pan, then blend each one to a puree with an immersion blender.
2. Pour 300 ml of boiling water over the couscous then cover and leave to steam for 5 minutes. Meanwhile, heat the oil in a frying pan and fry the vegetables and pine nuts for 5 minutes.
3. Fluff up the couscous grains with a fork and stir in the vegetables and parsley and transfer the mixture to a baking dish. Spread the broccoli puree on top, followed by the carrot puree, then sprinkle with cheese. Bake the gratin for 30 minutes or until golden brown.

Pan-fried Sea Bass with Chinese Artichokes

½ butternut squash, cut into chunks
200 g / 7 oz Chinese artichokes, scrubbed
2 tbsp olive oil
4 portions of sea bass fillet
2 tbsp butter
2 courgettes (zucchini), cut into chunks
100 g / 3 ½ oz chestnut mushrooms, halved
50 g / 1 ¾ oz / ⅓ cup walnuts

1. Preheat the oven to 180°C (160° fan) / 350F / gas 4 and put a roasting tin in to heat.
2. Boil the butternut squash in salted water for 3 minutes, then add the Chinese artichokes and cook for a further 4 minutes. Drain well.
3. Heat the oil in a frying pan and fry the sea bass skin side down for 3 minutes. Transfer the fillets, skin side up to the roasting tin in the oven and cook for 5 minutes.
4. Meanwhile, put the frying pan back on the hob and add the butter.
5. Fry the drained squash and artichokes with the courgette and mushrooms for 5 minutes, then stir in the walnuts and season. Divide the vegetables between four warm plates and top each one with a portion of sea bass.

Creamy Pea Soup

2 tbsp olive oil
2 tbsp low-fat butter
1 onion, finely chopped
2 garlic cloves, crushed
400 g / 14 oz peas, defrosted if frozen
1 litre / 1 pint 15 fl. oz / 4 cups
    vegetable stock
100 ml / 3 ½ fl. oz / ½ cup light cream
1 tbsp mint leaves, finely chopped

1. Heat the oil and butter in a saucepan and fry the onion for 5 minutes or until softened.
2. Add the garlic and peas to the pan and cook for 2 more minutes, then stir in the vegetable stock and bring to the boil.
3. Simmer for 5 minutes then stir in the double cream and mint.
4. Blend the soup until smooth with a liquidizer or immersion blender then try the soup and adjust the seasoning with salt and pepper.
5. Ladle into warm bowls and sprinkle with black pepper.

Mini Salmon Pies

2 tbsp low-fat butter
1 tsp plain (all purpose) flour
250 ml / 9 fl. oz / 1 cup skimmed milk
200 g / 7 oz salmon fillet, cubed
2 tbsp chives, chopped
250 g / 9 oz light puff pastry
1 egg, beaten

1. Preheat the oven to 200°C (180° fan) / 400F / gas 6.
2. Heat the butter in a saucepan then stir in the flour and cook for 30 seconds.
3. Gradually incorporate the milk, stirring all the time, then bring to a gentle simmer.
4. Stir in the salmon, then season with salt and pepper and divide the mixture between 4 mini casserole dishes.
5. Roll out the pastry on a lightly floured surface and cut out 4 circles.
6. Top each dish with a pastry lid and press round the edges to seal.
7. Brush the tops with beaten egg then bake for 25-30 minutes or until the pastry is golden brown and puffy.

Bruschetta with Ham

2 slices of sourdough bread, toasted
1 tsp wholegrain mustard
1 lemon, juiced
2 tsp extra virgin olive oil
1 tomato sliced
½ white onion, sliced
1 green chilli (chili), sliced
80 g / 3 oz Bresaola ham
sea salt and black pepper

1. Place the bread onto a serving plate. Combine the mustard, lemon juice and oil and whisk together before drizzling over the toasted bread.
2. Arrange the sliced tomato, onion and chilli on top of the bruschetta before topping with the ham and a little seasoning.

SERVES: 2 | PREP TIME: 15 MINS | MARINATE: 1 HOUR | COOKING TIME: 20 MINS

Chicken Burrito Bowl

1 tsp ground cumin

1 tsp ground coriander

1 tsp paprika

1 tsp chilli powder

½ tsp salt

1 tbsp olive oil

2 lemons, juiced.

2 large organic chicken breast

2 little gem lettuce, roughly chopped

100 g / 3 ½ oz / ½ cup long grain rice, cooked and drained

200 g / 7 oz black beans, cooked and drained

200 g / 7 oz sweetcorn, drained

2 large tomatoes, chopped

1 red onion, diced

a handful of fresh coriander (cilantro), chopped

1. In a large bowl, combine all the dried spices and salt with the oil and half the lemon juice to create a marinade. Trim the chicken breasts before adding to the marinade and coating. Cover and place in the refrigerator for at least an hour.

2. Preheat the oven to 180°C (160°C fan) / 350F / gas 4. Remove the chicken from the refrigerator at least 20 minutes before cooking.

3. Place on a non-stick baking tray and cook in the oven for around 20 minutes, or until the juices run clear at the thickest part of the meat when pierced with a knife.

4. In a large serving bowl, arrange the lettuce leaves before topping with the rice, which has had the beans mixed through it. Top with the sliced chicken breast. Combine the remaining ingredients in a bowl with the remaining lemon juice and season to taste.

5. Scatter around and over the chicken and serve.

Fusilli Puttanesca

75 g / 2 ½ oz fusilli pasta

1 tbsp olive oil

1 shallot, finely chopped

1 clove of garlic, minced

1 tsp chilli (chili) flakes

200 g / 7 oz passata

180 g / 6 ½ oz tinned tuna, in spring water

a handful of black olives, halved
    and deseeded

1 tbsp capers

Parmesan or Pecorino cheese to garnish

1. Bring a pan of salted water to the boil, add the pasta and cook for 10-12 minutes until cooked slightly al dente. Drain and set aside.
2. Heat the oil over a medium heat in a frying pan. Add the shallot and cook for 1 minute before adding the garlic and cooking for a further 30 seconds. Add the chilli, passata, tuna, olives and capers to the pan and simmer for 4-5 minutes until fragrant.
3. Add the pasta to your serving plate and spoon over the tuna sauce, garnish with a little grated cheese.

Beef in Red Wine

1 tbsp olive oil

450 g / 15 oz extra lean beef, diced

flour for dusting

1 onion, diced

2 garlic cloves, minced

150 ml / 5 fl. oz red wine

150 ml / 5 fl. oz beef stock

2 bay leaves

sprigs of fresh thyme

1. In a large casserole, heat the oil over a medium high heat. Season the beef and then brown in the oil. Remove with a slotted spoon at set aside, dusting with flour to catch the juices.
2. Add the onion to the pan and cook for 8 minutes until soft and translucent. Add the garlic and cook for a further minute before adding the wine to the pan. Allow this to bubble away until the liquid has reduced by half. Pour in the beef stock and return the beef to the pan with the bay leaves and thyme. Bring back to the boil and then reduce to a gentle simmer and cook for at least 1 hour, uncovered, until the beef is soft and the sauce has thickened.
3. Serve with vegetables.

Baked Mexican Eggs

2 tbsp olive oil
1 onion, diced
2 red chillies (chilies), deseeded
  finely chopped
2 red peppers, deseeded finely sliced
1 tsp smoked paprika
1 tsp cayenne powder
1 tsp cumin powder
200 g / 7 oz mushrooms, sliced
400 g / 14 oz chopped tomatoes, canned
400 g / 14 oz tin of kidney beans, drained
3 wholemeal tortilla wraps
300 ml / 10 fl. oz low-fat soured cream
4 free range eggs

1. Preheat oven to 180°C (160°C fan) / 350F / gas 4. In a pan, heat half the oil over a medium high heat, frying the onion for 3-4 minutes until translucent. Add the chillies, frying for a minute before adding the pepper, paprika, cayenne, cumin and mushrooms. Cook for a further 3 minutes, before adding the tomatoes. Turn down to a simmer and cook for 15 minutes, adding the beans for the final 5 minutes.

2. In a large ovenproof pan, heat the remaining oil. Fry each tortilla wrap for a minute on each side until browned. Remove from the heat and arrange all three in the pan. Spoon the tomato and bean mixture into the pan leaving room at the top.

3. Pour the soured cream over the top, ensuring a level surface, before cracking the eggs on top. Place in the oven for 10 minutes or until the eggs are cooked. Remove from the oven and garnish with fresh chilli and coriander.

Hot Dog Pizza

100 g / 3 ½ oz / ⅔ cup strong white flour
100 g / 3 ½ oz / ⅔ cup strong
  wholewheat flour
1 tsp easy-blend dried yeast
125ml / 4 fl. oz warm water
200ml / 6 ½ fl. oz passata
1 tsp dried oregano
150 g / 5 oz light mozzarella cheese
1 shallot, finely sliced
a handful of cherry tomatoes, halved
1 red chilli (chili), sliced
2 chicken or quorn hot dogs, sliced
a sprig of basil
chilli (chili) oil to drizzle

1. Combine the flours, yeast and a pinch of salt in a bowl. Pour in the water and knead for 5 minutes. Roll out on a floured surface and place onto an oiled baking tray.

2. With a ladle, spoon the passata onto the dough and spread evenly, leaving a little space at the edges. Tear the cheese into pieces and scatter over the pizza. Place the tomatoes, shallot, chilli and hot dogs over the pizza and drizzle with a little oil Leave to rise for 20 minutes. Meanwhile, preheat the oven to 240°C (220°C fan) / 475F / gas 9.

3. Once risen, place into the oven and cook for 12-15 minutes until the base is crisp and cheese has started to brown in places.

4. Scatter with chopped basil and serve.

MAKES: 1 | PREP TIME: 15 MINS | COOKING TIME: 30 MINS

Roast Vegetable Pizza

100 g / 3 ½ oz / ⅔ cup strong white flour
100 g / 3 ½ oz / ⅔ cup strong wholewheat flour
1 tsp easy-blend dried yeast
a pinch of salt
125ml / 4 fl. oz warm water
1 tsp olive oil
½ red onion, roughly chopped
1 courgette (zucchini), sliced
1 pepper, deseeded and sliced
100 g / 3 ½ oz mushrooms, roughly chopped
4 garlic cloves, lightly crushed
1 tsp each of oregano, basil and chilli (chili flakes)
1 tbsp low-fat pesto
150 g / 5 oz ricotta cheese
1 egg

1. Preheat oven to 180°C (160°C fan) / 350F / gas 4. Combine the flours, yeast and salt in bowl of a stand mixer. Mix using the dough hook, gradually add the water and oil until a soft dough forms.
2. Knead on a floured surface for a further minute, place into a lightly oiled bowl and cover with cling film to prove.
3. Combine the chopped vegetables, garlic, oregano, basil and chilli flakes with a drizzle of oil. Toss to coat and place onto a baking tray in the oven for 15-20 minutes until softened and slightly charred and remove.
4. Turn the heat up to 240°C (220°C fan) / 475F / gas 9. Turn out the dough and knock it back. Roll out to the desired shape and toss the vegetables with the pesto. Top the pizza dough with the roasted vegetables and add the ricotta, break the egg into the centre of the pizza.
5. Place into the oven on a baking tray for 15 minutes until the base is crisp and the cheese has started to brown.

SERVES: **2** | PREP TIME: **20 MINS** | COOKING TIME: **25 MINS**

Baked Chicken with Raw Salad

1 tbsp olive oil

1 tsp cumin seeds

1 tsp fennel seeds

1 tsp dried oregano

4 chicken drumsticks, or thighs

1 courgette (zucchini), halved lengthways and finely sliced

400 g / 14 oz cooked chickpeas, drained

½ red onion, finely sliced

200 g / 7 oz sweetcorn, drained

1 tbsp red wine vinegar

4 tbsp extra virgin olive oil

1 lemon, juiced

A small bunch of fresh parsley, chopped

1 little gem lettuce

a handful of cherry tomatoes

1. Preheat the oven to 200°C (180°C fan) / 400F / gas 6. in a bowl combine the oil, cumin seeds, fennel seeds and oregano and season. Add the chicken to the bowl and mix around in the marinade to coat the chicken. Place into an oven proof dish and bake in the oven for 20-25 minutes until golden.

2. While the chicken is cooking, add the courgette, chickpeas, red onion and sweet corn to a bowl. In a small jar with a lid, mix together the vinegar, oil and lemon and shake well to combine. Season with salt and pepper to taste. Pour this mixture over the mixed vegetables, adding the parsley, and toss to coat.

3. In a serving bowl, arrange the lettuce leaves and top with the vegetables, cooked chicken and tomatoes. Drizzle with a little oil and season to taste.

SERVES: **4** | PREP TIME: **10 MINS** | COOKING TIME: **45 MINS TO 1 HOUR**

Chilli Con Carne

1 tbsp olive oil

1 large onion, diced

2 red peppers, deseeded and diced

500 g / 1 lb lean beef mince

1 tsp chilli powder

1 tsp smoked paprika

1 tsp ground cumin

1 tsp ground coriander

400 g / 14 oz tinned chopped tomatoes

200 ml / 6 ½ fl. oz water

400 g / 14 oz tinned kidney beans, drained

low-fat soured cream

1. Heat the oil over a medium high heat in a large casserole. Add the onion and peppers and cook for 5-10 minutes until softened. Add the beef mince and brown before adding the chilli powder, paprika, cumin and coriander. Fry for a further minute until fragrant before adding the chopped tomatoes and water. Bring to the boil and then reduce to a simmer and cover and cook for 45 minutes.
2. Add the kidney beans to the chilli around 10 minutes before serving to heat through.
3. Serve in a bowl topped with a large spoonful of soured cream.

SERVES: 2 | PREP TIME: 10 MINS | COOKING TIME: 15 MINS

Chicken Burger

2 tbsp sunflower oil
2 chicken breast fillets
1 egg, beaten
50 g / 1 ¾ oz / ⅓ cup panko breadcrumbs
1 tbsp low-fat mayonnaise
½ lemon, juiced
1 tsp fresh dill, chopped
a pinch of salt
2 seeded burger buns

1. Preheat the oven to 180°C (160°C fan) / 350F / gas 4.
2. In a large frying pan, heat the oil over a medium high heat. Dip the chicken fillets into the beaten egg and then roll in the breadcrumbs until coated. Place the fillets into the heated oil and fry lightly on both sides until slightly golden. Remove from the pan and place onto a baking tray and bake in the oven for 10 minutes.
3. Combine the mayonnaise, lemon juice, dill and salt. Place the cooked chicken into the buns and top with the flavoured mayonnaise.

SERVES: 1 | PREP TIME: 10 MINS

Tuna Bruschetta

180 g / 6 ½ oz tuna, tinned in water

1 tsp capers, chopped

2 spring onions (scallions), chopped

1 lemon, juice and zest

1 tsp extra virgin olive oil

2 slices of ciabatta or baguette, toasted

1 garlic clove, peeled

a handful of fresh parsley, chopped

1. In a bowl, mix together the tuna, capers, spring onions, lemon and olive oil. Combine fully and season with salt and black pepper to taste.

2. Rub the toasted bread with the garlic clove to flavour.

3. Top with the tuna mixture and chopped parsley before serving.

SERVES: 6-8 | PREP TIME: 25 MINS | COOKING TIME: 40-50 MINS

Red Onion Savoury Cheesecake

200 g / 7 oz light puff pastry

3 tbsp olive oil

3 red onions, halved and sliced

450 g / 1 lb / 2 cups cream cheese

100 g / 3 ½ oz soft blue cheese, cubed

50 g / 1 ¾ oz / ½ cup pistachio nuts, chopped

1. Preheat the oven to 220°C (200° fan) / 425F / gas 7 and grease a baking tray.

2. Roll out the pastry on a lightly floured surface. Invert a large loaf tin on top of the pastry and cut round it, then transfer the pastry to the baking tray and prick with a fork.

3. Bake the pastry for 15 minutes or until golden brown and cooked through. Leave to cool.

4. Heat the oil in a large sauté pan and fry the onions over a gentle heat for 20 minutes, stirring occasionally.

5. Line the loaf tin with clingfilm then spoon in the onions and level the top.

6. Beat the cream cheese with the blue cheese and half of the pistachio nuts and spread it over the onions, then scatter over the rest of the pistachios.

7. Put the pastry on top, press down firmly and cover with clingfilm, then chill in the fridge for 3 hours before unmoulding and slicing.

SERVES: 2 | PREP TIME: 20 MINS | COOKING TIME: 20 MINS

Vegetable Bean Soup

1 tbsp olive oil
2 echalion shallots, diced
1 celery sticks, finely sliced
1 carrots, diced
2 garlic cloves, minced
½ cauliflower, florets only
1 tsp Herbes de Provence
750 ml / 25 fl. oz vegetable stock
1 bay leaf
240 g / 8 ½ oz can of cannellini beans, drained and rinsed
4 slices of crusty wholemeal bread
30 g parmesan, finely grated
curly leaf parsley to garnish

1. In a large saucepan or casserole dish, heat the oil over a medium high heat. Add the shallots, celery and carrots and cook for 4-5 minutes until fragrant and softened but not browned. Add the garlic, cauliflower and Herbes de Provence and fry for a further 2 minutes until fragrant.
2. Pour in the stock, season and bring to the boil. Reduce the heat to a simmer and cover, cooking for 15 minutes before adding the beans. Cook for a further 5 minutes.
3. Once you have added the beans, toast one side of the bread under a grill before turning over and sprinkling over the parmesan. Grill the other side until the cheese has browned.
4. Serve the hot soup in bowls with the parmesan toast on the side and garnish with chopped fresh parsley.

Desserts

MAKES: 6 | PREP TIME: 5 MINS | COOKING TIME: 5 MINS

Banana, Pear and Chocolate Pots

200 ml / 7 fl. oz / ¾ cup light cream

200 g / 7 oz dark chocolate, minimum 60% cocoa solids, chopped

3 bananas, sliced

2 pears, cored and diced

100 g / 3 ½ oz amaretti biscuits, crushed

1. Heat the cream until it starts to simmer, then pour it over the chopped chocolate and stir until the mixture has cooled and thickened.
2. Layer the chocolate ganache with the banana and pear inside 6 glass mugs and top with a sprinkle of crushed amaretti biscuits.

MAKES: 6 | PREP TIME: 5 MINS | COOKING TIME: 10 MINS | COOLING: 1 HOURS

Lime and Vanilla Stewed Pineapple

150 ml / 5 ½ fl. oz / ⅔ cup pineapple juice
1 lime, juiced and zest thinly pared
1 vanilla pod, split lengthways
1 pineapple, peeled, cored and cut into chunks
3 tbsp runny honey
coconut ice cream to serve

1. Put all of the ingredients in a saucepan and bring to a gentle simmer.
2. Stew the pineapple for 10 minutes, then leave to cool completely.
3. Serve with scoops of coconut ice cream.

MAKES: **1** | PREP TIME: **30 MINS** | COOKING TIME: **4 HOURS OR OVERNIGHT**

Vanilla Cheesecake

FOR THE BASE
100 g / 3 ½ oz / ¾ cup pecans
200 g / 7 oz Medjool dates
100 g / 3 ½ oz almond butter

FOR THE FILLING
600 g / 1 lb 3 oz light cream cheese
100 g / 3 ½ oz / 1 cup icing sugar
2 vanilla pods, seeds only
300 ml / 10 fl. oz low-fat crème fraîche
dark chocolate sauce, to serve

1. Place four 8 cm (3 in) pastry rings onto greaseproof paper on a baking tray.
2. In a food processor, blend together the pecans, dates and almond butter. Press into a large cheesecake ring and place in the fridge while you make the filling.
3. Mix the cream cheese, icing sugar and vanilla seeds in a mixer at a medium speed. Gradually add the crème fraiche until combined.
4. Spoon onto the cheesecake base and even out with a spatula. Refrigerate for at least 4 hours or overnight to set.
5. Remove from the fridge about 30 minutes before serving to come up to room temperature.
6. To remove the mould, place on top of a can and gently pull down the mould (heat the mould slightly, if necessary).
7. After slicing the cheesecake into wedges, drizzle with dark chocolate sauce to serve.
8. Delicious served with fresh berries.

MAKES: 6 | PREP TIME: 35 MINS | COOKING TIME: 10 MINS

Trifle Pots

300 g / 10 ½ oz raspberry Swiss roll, sliced
100 g / 3 ½ oz / ⅔ cup strawberries, sliced
100 g / 3 ½ oz / ⅔ cup blueberries
100 g / 3 ½ oz / ⅔ cup raspberries
4 tbsp sherry
300 ml / 10 ½ fl. oz / 1 ¼ cups light cream

FOR THE CUSTARD
450 ml / 12 ½ fl. oz / 1 ¾ cups
    skimmed milk
1 vanilla pod, split lengthways
4 large egg yolks
75 g / 2 ½ oz / ⅓ cup caster (superfine) sugar
1 tsp cornflour (cornstarch)

1. Layer the Swizz roll and fruit inside 6 glasses and drizzle over the sherry.
2. Combine the milk and vanilla pod in a saucepan and bring to simmering point.
3. Meanwhile, whisk the egg yolks with the caster sugar and cornflour until thick.
4. Gradually incorporate the hot milk, whisking all the time, then scrape the mixture back into the saucepan.
5. Stir the custard over a low heat until it thickens then spoon it into the glasses.
6. Leave the custard to cool to room temperature then whip the cream until it forms soft peaks and spoon it on top of the trifles.

SERVES: 6 | PREP TIME: 15 MINS | COOKING TIME: 25 MINS

Summer Fruit and Mint Crumbles

200 g / 7 oz / 1 ⅓ cups raspberries
200 g / 7 oz / 1 ⅓ cups blueberries
4 tbsp caster (superfine) sugar
3 sprigs of mint
75 g / 2 ½ oz / ⅓ cup low-fat butter
50 g / 1 ¾ oz / ⅓ cup plain
    (all purpose) flour
25 g / 1 oz / ¼ cup ground almonds

1. Preheat the oven to 180°C (160° fan) / 350F / gas 4.
2. Put the raspberries, blueberries, caster sugar and mint in a saucepan and cover it with a lid.
3. Heat gently for 5 minutes to soften the fruit and infuse it with mint, then discard the mint and divide the fruit between six individual baking dishes.
4. Rub the butter into the flour and stir in the ground almonds.
5. Crumble the mixture over the fruit then bake for 25 minutes or until the topping is golden brown.

Pear and Plum Tarte Tatin

3 tbsp low-fat butter, softened and cubed
2 tbsp manuka honey
4 pears, peeled, cored and quartered
12 small plums, stoned
6 mirabelles, stoned
250 g / 9 oz light puff pastry

1. Preheat the oven to 220°C (200° fan) / 425F / gas 7.
2. Dot the butter and manuka honey over the base of a large ovenproof frying pan.
3. Arrange the pears round the outside of the pan, followed by a ring of plums and the mirabelles in the centre.
4. Roll out the pastry on a floured surface and cut out a circle the same size as the frying pan.
5. Lay the pastry over the fruit and tuck in the edges, then transfer the pan to the oven and bake for 25 minutes or until the pastry is golden brown and cooked through.
6. Using oven gloves, put a large plate on top of the frying pan and turn them both over in one smooth movement to unmould the tart.

Fruits of the Forest Crumble

450 g / 1 lb / 3 cups mixed forest fruits
  (defrosted if frozen)
3 tbsp manuka honey
75 g / 2 ½ oz / ⅓ cup low-fat butter
50 g / 1 ¾ oz / ⅓ cup plain
  (all purpose) flour
25 g / 1 oz / ¼ cup ground almonds

1. Preheat the oven to 180°C (160° fan) / 350F / gas 4.
2. Mix the forest fruits with the manuka honey and arrange in an even layer in the bottom of a baking dish.
3. Rub the butter into the flour and stir in the ground almonds.
4. Squeeze a handful of the mixture into a clump and then crumble it over the fruit. Use up the rest of the topping in the same way, then shake the dish to level the top.
5. Bake the crumble for 40 minutes or until the topping is brown and the fruit is hot and bubbling.

MAKES: 12 | PREP TIME: **10 MINS** | COOKING TIME: **20 MINS**

Muffins with Chia Seeds

3 lemon, zest and juice
4 tbsp xylitol
300 g self raising flour
2 tbsp chia seeds
250 ml almond milk
60 g / 2 oz / ¼ cup low-fat butter, melted
2 large free range eggs, beaten

1. Preheat the oven to 200°C (180°C fan) / 400F / gas 6 and lightly grease a muffin tin.
2. Combine the lemon zest and xylitol together and mix thoroughly. Add the flour and chia seeds and mix well.
3. In a separate bowl, whisk together the almond milk, butter, lemon juice and egg until light. Make a well in the centre of the dry ingredients and pour in the egg mixture. Stir just enough to combine, not any more, as this will affect the texture.
4. Spoon the mixture into the muffin tin in equal amounts and place into the oven for 20-25 minutes until a skewer inserted into the centre comes out clean.
5. Remove from the tin and allow to cool before serving.

Pumpkin Cupcakes

150 g / 5 oz pumpkin, sliced
150 g / 5 oz / 1 cup plain flour
1 tsp cinnamon
½ tsp ground ginger
½ tsp ground allspice
1 tbsp baking powder
1 tsp bicarbonate soda
100 g / 3 ½ oz / ½ cup low-fat butter
2 tbsp manuka honey
2 eggs
100 ml / 3 ½ fl. oz skimmed milk
150 g / 5 oz low-fat cream cheese
150 g icing sugar
1 tsp vanilla extract
pumpkin seeds

1. Preheat oven to 200°C (180°C fan) / 400F / gas 6 and place the sliced pumpkin into the oven for 20 minutes until soft. Remove and when cooled remove the flesh and blend into a puree in a food processor or blender.
2. Place 12 muffin cases into a muffin tin, or lightly grease a muffin tin. Combine the flour, spices, baking powder and bicarbonate of soda in a large mixing bowl.
3. In a separate bowl, combine half the butter and manuka honey. Add the eggs, one at a time, and mix. Stir in the milk and pumpkin puree using a wooden spoon, followed by the flour mixture.
4. Spoon the mixture into the muffin cases and bake for 30 minutes until light and bouncy. Cool in the tin before removing to a wire rack.
5. Combine the cream cheese and remaining butter and beat until smooth. Gradually add the icing sugar then vanilla extract and mix until light.
6. Ice the cakes once cooled and sprinkle over some pumpkin seeds.

Dairy-free Almond Butter Cookies

200 g / 7 oz almond butter
150 g / 5 oz / ¾ cup light brown sugar
1 egg
1 tsp vanilla extract
50 g / 1 ¾ oz / ½ cup ground almonds
sea salt for sprinkling

1. Preheat the oven to 200°C (180°C fan) / 400F / gas 6 and line a baking tray with grease proof paper. In a bowl, mix together the almond butter, sugar, egg and vanilla extract. Once combined stir in the ground almonds until you have a stiff dough.
2. Using your hand roll pieces of the dough into a ball the size of a cherry tomato. Flatten and place onto the baking tray and sprinkle with sea salt.
3. Place into the oven and bake for 10 minutes until lightly golden. Remove to cool on the tray for 5 minutes and then a wire rack to cool completely.

SERVES: 8 | PREP TIME: 30 MINS | COOKING TIME: 2 HOURS

Pear Frangipane Tarts

2 ripe pears
2 tbsp honey
2 lemons, juice and zest
100 ml / 3 ½ fl. oz water
1 cinnamon stick

FOR THE BASE
200 g / 7 oz / 1 ⅓ cups plain flour
100 g / 3 ½ oz / ½ cup low-fat butter
1 egg

FOR THE FILLING
75 g / 2 ½ oz / ⅓ cup low-fat butter
75 g / 2 ½ oz / ⅓ cup caster sugar
2 eggs, beaten
75 / 2 ½ oz / ¾ cup ground almonds
1 tsp vanilla extract

1. Preheat the oven to 190°C (170°C fan) / 375F / gas 5. Cut the bottom off the pears and stand in an oven proof dish. Mix the honey, lemon juice and water and pour over the pears, add the cinnamon. Bake for an hour basting with the syrup every 15 minutes. They should be slightly soft when ready, remove to cool.

2. Lightly grease a 28 cm loose bottomed fluted tart tin. Add the flour and butter into a food processor and pulse until it resembles breadcrumbs. Add the egg and a drop of water mixing until the dough forms.

3. Roll out the pastry on a floured surface as thinly as possible and place into the tart tin. Prick with a fork and set aside.

4. Make the frangipane by whisking the sugar and butter until creamy. Mix in the eggs, followed by the ground almonds and vanilla extract. Spoon into the tart base. Slice the pears and arrange on top.

5. Place on a baking tray and bake for 50 minutes until the pastry is crisp and tart is golden brown.

MAKES: 4 | PREP TIME: 15 MINS | COOKING TIME: 40 MINS

Mini Pear Quinoa Crumbles

200 g / 7 oz / 1 cup quinoa

1 cinnamon stick

4 pears, peeled and cubed

1 tbsp manuka honey

50 g / 1 ¾ oz / ¼ cup low-fat butter, melted

50 g / 1 ¾ oz / ½ cup ground almonds

75 g / 2 ½ oz / ½ cup dark brown sugar

1. Preheat the oven to 200°C (180° fan) / 400F / gas 6.
2. Put the quinoa and cinnamon in a saucepan with 450 ml water and bring to the boil. Cover the pan, then reduce the heat and simmer gently for 15 minutes or until all the water has been absorbed.
3. Spread the quinoa out onto a tray and leave to steam dry for a few minutes.
4. Toss the pears with the manuka honey and divide them between four individual baking dishes.
5. Stir the melted butter, ground almonds and brown sugar into the quinoa, then sprinkle the mixture on top of the pears.
6. Bake the crumbles in the oven for 25 minutes or until the tops are golden brown.

Small Summer Berry Crumbles

200 g / 7 oz / 1 ⅓ cups raspberries
200 g / 7 oz / 1 ⅓ cups strawberries, halved
2 tbsp manuka honey
75 g / 2 ½ oz / ⅓ cup low-fat butter
50 g / 1 ¾ oz / ⅓ cup plain (all purpose) flour
25 g / 1 oz / ¼ cup ground almonds
40 g / 1 ½ oz / ¼ cup light
   brown sugar

1. Preheat the oven to 180°C (160° fan) / 350F / gas 4.
2. Mix the raspberries and strawberries with the manuka honey and divide them between six ramekin dishes.
3. Rub the butter into the flour and stir in the ground almonds and brown sugar.
4. Crumble the mixture over the fruit then bake for 25 minutes or until the topping is golden brown.

Crispy Marshmallow Squares

2 tbsp coconut oil
1 tsp vanilla extract
250 g / 9 oz sugar free marshmallows
150 g / 5 oz puffed rice
100 g / 3 ½ oz dark chocolate (min.
   70% cocoa solids)

1. Lightly grease a 22 x 33 cm (9 x 13 in) tin and set aside.
2. In a large saucepan, add the coconut oil and heat gently to melt, stirring in the vanilla extract. Add the marshmallows and gently melt then stirring all the time. Once melted add the puffed rice and completely mix into the marshmallow. Quickly transfer to the prepared tin ensuring that it is even and flat across the whole tin.
3. Leave to set for 2 hours before cutting into 16 cubes.
4. Before serving, melt the chocolate in a heatproof bowl over simmering water. Drizzle across the marshmallow cubes using a spoon.

SERVES: **6** | PREP TIME: **15 MINS** | COOKING TIME: **25 MINS**

Raspberry Upside-down Cake

100 g / 3 ½ oz / ⅔ cup self-raising flour

1 tsp baking powder

100 g / 3 ½ oz / ½ cup caster (superfine) sugar

100 g / 3 ½ oz / ½ cup low-fat butter, softened

2 large eggs

250 g / 9 oz / 2 cups fresh raspberries

icing (confectioner's) sugar for dusting

1. Preheat the oven to 180°C (160° fan) / 350F / gas 4 and butter a 20 cm round cake tin.

2. Sieve the flour and baking powder into a mixing bowl and add sugar, butter and eggs.

3. Beat the mixture with an electric whisk for 4 minutes or until smooth and well whipped.

4. Arrange half of the raspberries in the cake tin and spoon the cake mixture on top.

5. Level the cake mixture with a palette knife and bake for 25 minutes or until a skewer inserted comes out clean.

6. Leave the cake to cool for 20 minutes before turning out onto a serving plate.

7. Top with the rest of the raspberries and sprinkle with icing sugar just before serving.

SERVES: 2 | PREP TIME: 10 MINS | CHILLING TIME: 30 MINS

Mango Dessert

1 mango, peeled and de-stoned
1 tsp fruit syrup
500 ml / 17 fl. oz low-fat Greek yogurt
fresh sliced strawberries, to garnish

1. Place the mango into a food processor and blend to a purée.
2. Place two thirds of the yogurt into the bottom of two serving glasses before adding a layer of mango purée. Top with the remaining yogurt and chill for 30 minutes or until needed.
3. Before serving, top with the sliced strawberries.

SERVES: 8-10 | PREP TIME: 45 MINS | COOKING TIME: 15 MINS

Lemon Meringue Pie

FOR THE BASE
100 g / 3 ½ oz / 1 cup ground almonds
1 egg, whisked
1 tbsp plain flour
¼ tsp stevia

FOR THE CURD
3 eggs
100 g / 3 ½ oz / ⅓ cup honey

1 lemon, juice and zest
80 g / 3 oz / ⅓ cup unsalted,
   low-fat butter

FOR THE MERINGUE
4 egg whites
¼ tsp cream of tartar
100 g / 3 ½ oz / ½ cup caster sugar

1. Preheat the oven to 200°C (180°C fan) / 400F / gas 6. Lightly grease a medium
   sized pie dish.
2. In a bowl, mix the almonds and egg, gradually adding the flour to form a non-sticky
   dough. Roll out and place into the pie dish, pushing into the corners and trimming
   off excess. Bake for 10 minutes until crisp.
3. For the curd, whisk the eggs and honey in a saucepan adding the lemon zest.
   Lower the heat and whisk until thickened and pale yellow. Add the lemon juice
   and butter, a little at a time, whisking until just starting to bubble. Pass through a
   sieve and set aside.
4. For the meringue, whisk the egg whites and tartar in a stand mixer on high until soft
   peaks form. Turn down the whisk and gradually add the sugar until thick and glossy.
5. Assemble the cake by spreading the cooled curd over the base and topping with
   the meringue. Place under a grill for 5 minutes or until the meringue has started to
   brown in places.

SERVES: 4 | PREP TIME: 10 MINS

Creamy Apple and Honey Dessert

200 g / 7 oz low-fat crème fraiche
150 g / 5 oz 0% fat greek yogurt
50 g / 1.7 oz / ¼ cup honey
2 meringue shells, crushed
1 apple, cored and sliced
1 tbsp bee pollen

1. In a bowl, fold together the crème fraiche, yogurt and honey.
2. Add the crushed meringue and mix through.
3. Spoon the mixture into serving glasses and top with apple slices and a small amount of bee pollen

Chocolate Orange Mousse

100 g / 3 ½ oz dark chocolate, 80% cocoa solids

1 tsp Cointreau

1 tbsp cocoa powder

1 orange, zest only

2 egg whites

1 tbsp sugar

50 g / 1 ¾ oz low-fat yogurt

1. Place a heat proof bowl of a pan of simmering water taking care it does not touch the water. Break up the chocolate and gently melt in the bowl adding the Cointreau, cocoa powder and 1 teaspoon of the orange zest. Remove from the heat as soon as it has melted and set aside.
2. Whisk the egg whites in a mixer until soft peaks form. Gradually add the sugar whilst continuing to whisk until it becomes thick and glossy.
3. Mix together the cooled melted chocolate with the yogurt until combined. Gently fold in a tablespoon of the egg using a metal spoon, before folding in the remaining egg without knocking out the air.
4. Spoon into serving glasses and chill for at least 4 hours or overnight.
5. Top with the remaining orange zest before serving.

Cranberry and Oat Muffins

150 g / 5 oz / 1 ½ cups rolled oats

100 g / 3 ½ oz / ½ cup self-raising flour

1 tsp baking powder

1 tsp cinnamon

100 g / 3 ½ oz / ½ cup light muscovado sugar

100 g / 3 ½ oz / ⅔ cup cranberries

1 lemon, zest

200 ml / 6 ½ fl. oz skimmed milk

3 tbsp sunflower oil

1 egg, lightly beaten

1. Preheat the oven to 180°C (160°C fan) / 350F / gas 4 and line a 12 hole tin with muffin cases. Place the oats into a blender and grind to a fine powder. Combine with the flour, baking powder, cinnamon, sugar, cranberries and lemon and mix.
2. In a separate bowl, mix the milk, oil and egg. Make a well in the centre of the dry ingredients and gradually pour in the milk and egg mixture. Mix just enough to combine the ingredients, no more, and spoon into the muffin cases. Bake in the oven for 20 minutes until risen and firm to touch.

SERVES: 8 | PREP TIME: 20 MINS | COOKING TIME: 1 HOUR

Almond Cake

200 g / 7 oz / ¾ cup low-fat butter
100 g / 7 oz / ¾ cup xylitol (or alternative low-calorie sweetener)
4 eggs
150 g / 5 oz / 1 ½ cups ground almonds
50 g / 1 ¾ oz / ⅓ cup plain flour
1 tsp almond extract
icing sugar for dusting

1. Preheat the oven to 180°C (160°C fan) / 350F / gas 4 and grease and line a 20 cm (8 in) cake tin.
2. Cream the butter and xylitol until light and fluffy. Gradually beat in the eggs, one at a time, before folding in the almonds, flour and almond extract.
3. Pour the mixture into the prepared cake tin and even out with a spatula. Bake in the centre of an oven for 1 hour, or until a skewer inserted into the centre of the cake comes out clean.
4. Remove from the oven and place on a wire rack to cool. Dust with icing sugar when ready to serve.

Snacks and Sides

SERVES: 4 | PREP TIME: 15 MINS | COOKING TIME: 45 MINS

Potato Wedges

800 g / 1 lb 12 oz potatoes, peeled and
  cut into wedges
1 tsp garlic powder
60 ml / 2 fl. oz / ¼ cup olive oil

1. Parboil the potatoes in boiling salted
   water for 5 minutes, then drain well
   and leave to steam dry for 2 minutes.

2. Meanwhile, put the oil in a large
   roasting tin in the oven and heat it to
   200°C (180°C fan) / 400F / gas 6.

3. Mix the garlic powder with ½
   teaspoon of salt and pepper, then
   sprinkle the mixture evenly over the
   potatoes. Carefully tip the wedges
   into the roasting tin and turn to coat
   in the oil.

4. Bake the wedges for 45 minutes,
   turning every 15 minutes, until
   golden brown on the outside and
   fluffy within.

5. Sprinkle with a little more salt and
   serve immediately.

SERVES: **4** | PREP TIME: **5 MINS** | COOKING TIME: **25 MINS**

Braised Spring Vegetables

2 tbsp olive oil

4 baby artichokes, halved

175 ml / 6 fl. oz / ⅔ cup dry white wine

2 leeks, cut into large chunks

8 shallots, peeled

12 small chantenay carrots, scrubbed

500 ml / 17 ½ fl. oz / 2 cups good quality vegetable stock

12 asparagus spears, trimmed

150 g / 5 ½ oz / 1 cup fresh peas

1 tbsp lemon juice

2 tbsp flat leaf parsley, finely chopped

1. Heat the oil in a large cast iron casserole dish and sear the cut sides of the artichokes until well browned.
2. Pour in the wine and bring to the boil, then add the leeks, shallots, carrots and stock and bring back to the boil.
3. Reduce the heat and simmer gently for 10 minutes, then add the asparagus and peas and simmer for a further 8 minutes.
4. Add a squeeze of lemon then season to taste with salt and pepper and sprinkle with parsley.

SERVES: 4 | PREP TIME: 20 MINS | COOKING TIME: 8 MINS

Gammon and Salad Onion Skewers

6 salad onions
400 g / 14 oz unsmoked gammon, cubed
4 tbsp barbecue sauce

1. Put 12 wooden skewers in a bowl of water and leave to soak for 20 minutes.
2. Meanwhile, cut off the green parts of the onions and reserve for garnish. Cut the bulb of the onions in half.
3. Thread the gammon and onions onto the skewers and spread them out on a large grill tray.
4. Brush them with barbecue sauce then grill for 4 minutes on each side or until the onions are slightly charred on the edges.
5. Slice the reserved onion greens on the diagonal and scatter over the skewers.

SERVES: 4 | PREP TIME: 15 MINS

Nacho Dip

2 red chillies (chili)

½ red onion

3 ripe avocados

2 garlic cloves, minced

1 bunch fresh coriander (cilantro)

6 cherry tomatoes

2 limes, juice and zest

himalayan sea salt

1. De-seed and finely chop the red chillies and finely dice the red onion.
2. Peel and de-stone the avocado and mash in a bowl with the back of a fork. Mix in the chopped chilli, garlic and onion.
3. Finely chop some of the coriander stalks and roughly chop the leaves before adding to the avocado along with the chopped and deseeded tomatoes. Add the lime juice and zest and season to taste with the salt.
4. Serve alongside plain tortilla chips for a great snack.

SERVES: 6 | PREP TIME: 20 MINS | COOKING TIME: 35 MINS

Spicy Lamb Samosas

2 tbsp olive oil

1 small onion, finely chopped

2 cloves of garlic, crushed

250 g / 9 oz / 1 cup minced lamb

¼ tsp chilli (chili) powder

½ tsp ground cumin

½ tsp ground coriander

¼ tsp ground cinnamon

50 g / 1 ¾ oz / ⅓ cup frozen peas, defrosted

225 g / 8 oz filo pastry

100 g / 3 ½ oz / ½ cup butter, melted

1. Preheat the oven to 180°C (160° fan) / 350F / gas 4 and grease a large baking tray.
2. Heat the oil in a frying pan and fry the onion for 5 minutes or until softened.
3. Add the garlic and minced lamb and cook for 5 more minutes then add the spices and peas. Turn off the heat and leave to cool for a few minutes.
4. Cut the pile of filo sheets in half then take one halved sheet and brush it with melted butter.
5. Arrange a tablespoon of the filling at one end and fold the corner over, then triangle-fold it up.
6. Transfer the samosa to the baking tray and repeat with the rest of the filo and filling, then brush with any leftover butter.
7. Bake the samosas for 20 minutes, turning half way through, until the pastry is crisp and golden brown.

SERVES: 4 | PREP TIME: 30 MINS | COOKING TIME: 45 MINS

Mushroom and Ricotta Parcels

2 tbsp olive oil

250 g / 9 oz Portobello mushrooms

2 garlic cloves, chopped

200 g / 7 oz spinach, washed

200 g / 7 oz low -fat ricotta cheese

3 sheets of filo pastry

1tbsp butter, melted

½ leek, cut into thin strips

1. Heat the oil in a large pan over a medium high heat. Cut the mushrooms into roughly 2 cm cubes and fry for 4 minutes until browned. Add the garlic and cook for 1 minute. Remove and set aside to cool.
2. Add the spinach and fry for 3 minutes until wilted. Remove onto kitchen paper, squeezing out as much liquid as possible. Roughly chop and add to the mushrooms.
3. Once cooled, mix the ricotta cheese into the mushrooms and spinach, seasoning to taste. Refrigerate until needed.
4. Preheat oven to 200°C (180°C fan) / 400F / gas 6. Cut the filo sheets into rough 20 cm (8 in) squares. Arrange three sheets on top of each other in a star shape brushing lightly with melted butter between each layer. Add a spoonful of the mushroom mixture in the centre of each star and bring up the edges to form a parcel. Tie the top using a thin strip of leek.
5. Place in the oven and bake for 15 minutes or until the pastry has turned golden brown.

SERVES: **2** | PREP TIME: **10 MINS** | COOKING TIME: **15 MINS**

Fish Bites with Tartar Sauce

100 g / 3 ½ oz light mayonnaise

1 tbsp capers, chopped

2 gherkins, chopped

½ shallot, finely diced

1 lemon, juice

a handful of dill, finely chopped

a handful of flat leaf parsley, chopped

100 g / 3 ½ oz / ⅔ cup plain flour

1 tsp turmeric

a pinch of salt

150 ml / 3 ½ fl. oz sparkling water

250 g / 9 oz white fish (such as cod or pollock), cut into chunks

flour for dredging the fish

sunflower oil for frying

1. Start by making the tartar sauce by mixing the mayonnaise with the capers, gherkins, shallot, lemon juice and herbs. Place in the fridge until required.
2. Combine the flour, turmeric and salt in a mixing bowl. Whisk together using a balloon whisk until smooth and no lumps are left.
3. Heat the oil in a deep fryer or in a wok to around 5 cm depth over a medium high heat, it will be hot enough when a drop of batter sizzles and crisps quickly when added to it. Dip the fish pieces into the flour and then the batter, allowing any excess to drip off. Place into the hot oil using a basket or slotted spoon and fry for around 5 minutes until golden. Remove and place onto kitchen paper to soak up any excess oil. Repeat until all the fish has been cooked.
4. Serve immediately with the tartar sauce and lemon wedges.

SERVES: 4 | PREP TIME: 10-15 MINS | COOKING TIME: 15-20 MINS

Traditional Stuffed Tomatoes

FOR THE TOMATOES

6 large vine tomatoes

600 g / 1 lb 5 oz / 4 cups beef mince

2 tbsp sunflower oil

2 cloves of garlic, minced

1 tsp dried oregano

1 tsp dried basil

salt and pepper

TO GARNISH

250 g / 9 oz / 1 ½ cups cooked white long grain rice

a few sprigs of oregano

1. Preheat the oven to 190°C (170° fan) / 375F / gas 5.
2. Heat the sunflower oil in a large sauté pan set over a moderate heat.
3. Sauté the garlic for 30 seconds before adding the beef mince.
4. Cook until browned all over before adding the dried herbs and seasoning to taste.
5. Remove to one side to cool as you prepare the tomatoes.
6. Remove their tops and reserve to one side before scooping out the seeds and flesh. Fill with the beef mince and replace their tops.
7. Spoon the rice into an oval baking dish and sprinkle with cold water.
8. Sit the stuffed tomatoes on top and bake for 10-12 minutes until warmed through.
9. Remove from the oven and garnish with oregano before serving.

SERVES: 4 | PREP TIME: 15 MINS | COOKING TIME: 45 MINS

Sweet Potato Wedges with Paprika

800 g / 1 lb 12 oz potatoes, cut into wedges with the skin left on
1 tsp smoked paprika
60 ml / 2 fl. oz / ¼ cup olive oil

1. Wash then parboil the sweet potatoes in boiling salted water for 5 minutes, then drain well and leave to steam-dry for 2 minutes.
2. Meanwhile, put the oil in a large roasting tin in the oven and heat it to 200°C (180°C fan) / 400F / gas 6.
3. Mix the smoked paprika with ½ a teaspoon of salt and pepper, then sprinkle the mixture evenly over the sweet potatoes.
4. Carefully tip the wedges into the roasting tin and turn to coat in the oil.
5. Bake the wedges for 45 minutes, turning every 15 minutes, until golden brown on the outside and fluffy within. Sprinkle with a little more salt and serve immediately.

Potato Salad

500 g / 1 lb baby potatoes, peeled
   and cubed

250 g / 8 ½ lbs / 1 cup low-fat greek
   yogurt

30 ml / 1 fl. oz extra virgin olive oil

1 tbsp capers

100 g / 3 ½ oz / ½ cup spring onions
   (scallions), finely sliced

a handful of fresh dill, finely chopped

sea salt and freshly ground black pepper

1. Place the potatoes into a pan of boiling salted water and cook for 15-20 minutes until just soft. Drain and set aside to cool.
2. Once cool combine the potatoes with the yogurt in a large bowl. Mix through the remaining ingredients and season to taste.
3. Serve as a side dish, ideal with cold meats or at a BBQ.

Onion Rings

2 onions, sliced into 1 cm thick rounds

400 ml / 13 ½ fl. oz low-fat buttermilk

140 g / 5 oz / 1 cup plain flour

½ tsp cayenne

300 ml / 10 fl. oz groundnut oil

50 g / 1 ¾ oz corn flour

180 ml / 6 fl. oz sparkling water

1. Place the sliced onions into a baking dish and cover with the buttermilk. Cover with cling film and leave at room temperature for up to an hour.
2. Put 100 g of the plain flour onto a plate with the cayenne and season. Drain the onions and coat them in the seasoned flour.
3. Heat the oil in a saucepan or fryer to 180°C / 350F. Meanwhile, make the batter by combining the remaining flour with the sparkling water and a pinch of salt and mix until smooth.
4. Dip each onion ring into the batter and fry in the oil for 3-4 minutes until crisp.
5. Remove when browned and place onto kitchen paper to dry and toss with salt.

MAKES: **6** | PREP TIME: **20 MINS**

Luxury Seafood and Avocado Cocktails

250 g / 9 oz sashimi-grade tuna loin, diced

2 tbsp soy sauce

1 tsp sesame oil

4 avocados, halved and stoned

2 limes, juiced

1 tsp wasabi paste

150 g / 5 ½ oz cooked crayfish tails, peeled

150 g / 5 ½ oz / ¾ cup white crabmeat

18 king prawns

250 g / 9 oz / 1 cup light mayonnaise

2 tbsp fresh dill, chopped, plus a few sprigs to garnish

cayenne pepper for sprinkling

1. Toss the tuna with the soy and sesame oil then divide between 6 glasses.
2. Scrape the avocado flesh out of the skins and put it in a food processor with the lime juice and wasabi paste. Blend to a smooth puree and add salt to taste.
3. Spoon the avocado mixture on top of the tuna and top with the crayfish tails and crabmeat.
4. Arrange 3 king prawns on top of each cocktail, then pipe or spoon some mayonnaise on top.
5. Sprinkle with dill and cayenne pepper and garnish with some extra sprigs of dill.

MAKES: **4** | PREP TIME: **1 HOUR** | COOKING TIME: **35–40 MINS**

Mini Vegetable Quiches

2 tbsp olive oil
1 small onion, finely chopped
1 large carrot, diced
1 courgette (zucchini), diced
3 large eggs
225 ml / 8 fl. oz / ¾ cup light cream

FOR THE PASTRY
100 g / 3 ½ oz / ½ cup low-fat
   butter, cubed
200 g / 7 oz / 1 ⅓ cups plain
   (all purpose) flour
1 large egg, beaten

1. To make the pastry, rub the butter into the flour until the mixture resembles fine breadcrumbs.
2. Stir in enough cold water to bring the pastry together into a pliable dough and chill for 30 minutes.
3. Preheat the oven to 190°C (170° fan) / 375F / gas 5.
4. Roll out the pastry on a floured surface and use it to line 4 individual tart cases.
5. Prick the pastry with a fork, line with greaseproof baking paper and fill with baking beans or rice.
6. Bake the cases for 10 minutes then remove the paper and baking beans.
7. Meanwhile, heat the oil in a frying pan and fry the onion, carrot and courgette for 5 minutes or until softened.
8. Gently whisk the eggs with the cream until smoothly combined then stir in the vegetables and season generously with salt and pepper.
9. Pour the filling into the pastry cases, then lower the oven temperature to 150°C (130° fan) / 300F / gas 2 and bake for 20 minutes or until just set in the centre.

Index